Plants and Trees Growing

by Kara Race-Moore

PEARSON
Scott
Foresman

Plants and Their Parts

Plants are amazing! Plants grow all over the Earth. There are many different types of plants. Plants are many different colors and sizes. They make many different types of flowers and seeds. There are many things that make plants different. Still, they all have several important things in common.

Cactus

Like animals, all plants need food, water, and space to grow. One of the reasons animals need space to move around is to find food. Plants don't need to find food. They are able to make their own food, using their special parts.

Tree

Water lily

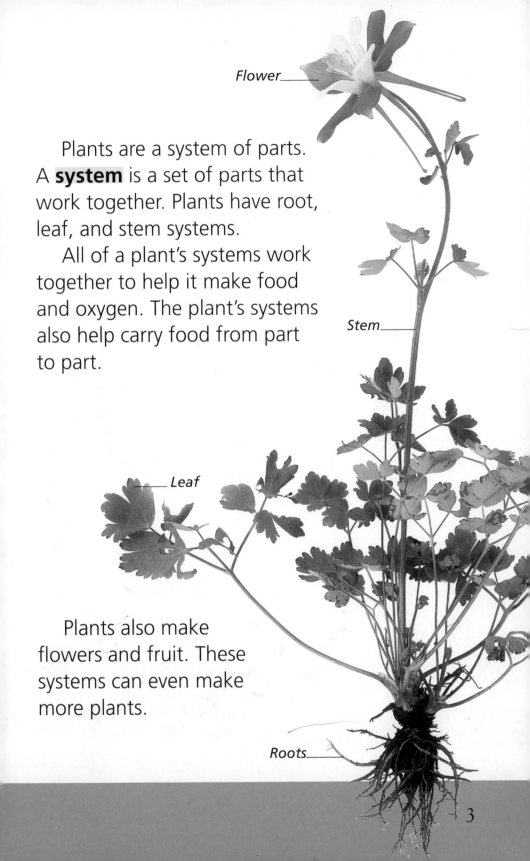

Flower

Plants are a system of parts. A **system** is a set of parts that work together. Plants have root, leaf, and stem systems.

All of a plant's systems work together to help it make food and oxygen. The plant's systems also help carry food from part to part.

Stem

Leaf

Plants also make flowers and fruit. These systems can even make more plants.

Roots

3

Plants Make Food

A plant's parts work together to make it grow. Plants can make their own food in order to live and grow. Different parts of the plant do different things to help the plant grow.

Roots get water from the ground. The roots and stem bring the water to the plant's leaves through tubes.

Flower

Stem

Roots

The leaves bring in carbon dioxide from the air. It enters through tiny holes on the bottom of the leaf. In the leaves, the plant uses energy from sunlight to change carbon dioxide and water into sugar and oxygen.

The plant uses the sugar to grow. It lets the oxygen out through tiny holes on the undersides of the leaves. Many other living things use the oxygen that plants make.

Leaves

Plant Roots

Roots make up an important plant system. The roots of a plant hold it in the ground and keep it steady. They take water and minerals from the soil to help the plant grow. Some plants also store food in their roots.

Radish

There are different types of roots. Carrot roots are a kind of taproot. A taproot grows deep into the soil. Smaller roots, called fibrous roots, grow off the main taproot. These roots are called fibrous roots because they look like slender fibers. People eat the taproots of carrots for food.

Carrot

As a tree grows taller, its branches grow out farther and farther. Smaller branches grow from the tree's main branches at the same time.

Tree roots grow in the soil in a similar way. They grow out as far as they can to get as much water and as many minerals as possible.

Inside the root are tubes. The tubes take the water and minerals to the stems and leaves.

Stems and Leaves

The stems support and connect all of the plant systems. Stems bring water and minerals from the roots to the leaves. Then the stems bring the sugars the leaves make back down to the roots to help them grow.

Different plants have different types of stems. Some stems grow thick to protect plants from the Sun. Other stems are covered in sharp thorns to prevent animals from eating the plants. Ivy stems are thin and flexible. They grow around other objects, such as trees or fence posts, for support.

Plants also have different types of leaves. Many evergreen trees have hard, skinny leaves that look like needles.

Pine needles

Trees, such as oaks and maples, have flat, broad, flexible leaves.

A leaf can be one piece. It can also be made of many leaflets growing off a main vein. A plant's leaves always grow in a pattern.

Oak leaves

Growing a Seed

A flowering plant grows from a single seed. Seeds are formed in the flower of a plant. To make seeds, a plant has to be pollinated. A plant will **pollinate** when pollen gets moved near the center of a flower to a part that makes seeds. Seeds then form in the middle of the flower.

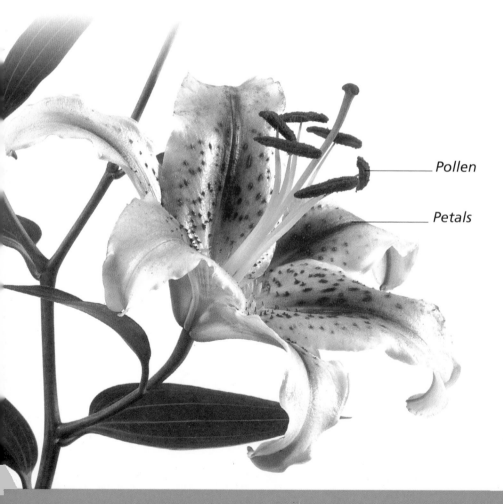

Pollen

Petals

A flower is made up of several parts. Its outside parts are called petals. Petals are often brightly colored to attract birds and insects. This helps with the pollination process. The wind can also carry pollen to polinate a plant.

Scattering Seeds

The wind does more than carry pollen to a plant's flowers. It can also blow seeds away from the parent plant. Dandelion seeds have a parachute design that allows the wind to blow them far and wide.

Dandelion flower

Dandelion seeds

Water can carry seeds that have strong seed coats. Those seeds can then grow in other places. Wind and water bring many seeds to islands that are far out in the sea.

Animals can also move seeds and pollen. Pollen and seeds can stick to an animal's fur or feathers when it brushes against a plant or eats its nectar. Those seeds then scatter as the animal walks or flies around.

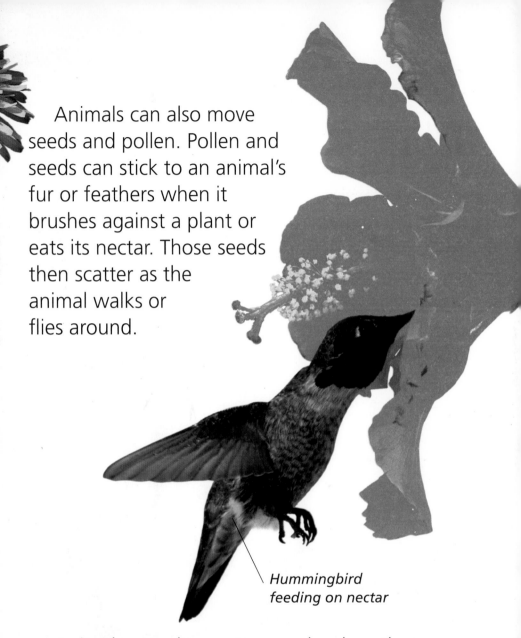

Hummingbird feeding on nectar

Animals can also scatter seeds when they eat a plant's fruit. The seeds pass through the animals' bodies after they eat the fruit.

Young Plants

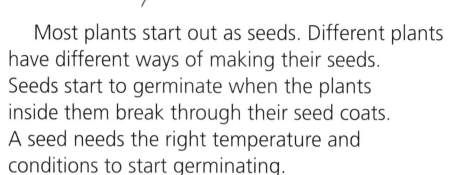

Most plants start out as seeds. Different plants have different ways of making their seeds. Seeds start to germinate when the plants inside them break through their seed coats. A seed needs the right temperature and conditions to start germinating. To **germinate** means to begin to grow.

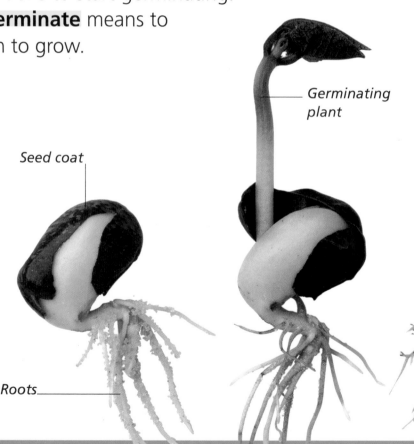

Germinating plant

Seed coat

Roots

The developing plant uses food that is stored inside the seed's **seed leaf** to grow.

New plants are called **seedlings.** Seedlings quickly grow roots and a stem. The roots and the stem allow seedlings to start making their own food after they have used up the seed leaf's food.

Seedlings start getting bigger, and soon their first true leaves start making food. After a while, seedlings make more leaves.

Deciduous And Coniferous

Trees are a kind of plant. Two types of trees are **deciduous** trees and **coniferous** trees. The leaves on deciduous trees fall off every year when the weather gets cold. Deciduous trees grow new leaves in the spring, when the weather gets warm again. Coniferous trees shed and replace their leaves throughout the year.

Deciduous trees are flowering plants. They grow their seeds inside things like fruits and nuts. Oak, apple, and maple trees are deciduous trees.

Coniferous trees do not have flowers. They grow seeds in cones. Pine, spruce, and fir trees are coniferous trees.

Cones

Coniferous trees grow two types of cones. The small cones make pollen. The large cones can grow seeds. A coniferous tree gets pollinated when the wind blows pollen from the small cones to the large cones.

The seeds inside the large cones ripen. Cones with ripe seeds fall to the ground. Then the seeds can germinate in the soil.

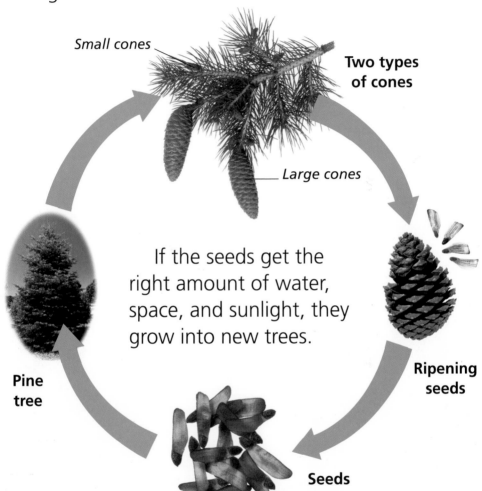

Small cones

Two types of cones

Large cones

If the seeds get the right amount of water, space, and sunlight, they grow into new trees.

Pine tree

Ripening seeds

Seeds

Later, the new trees will make their own large and small cones. When that happens, the life cycle of the evergreen trees will start again.

Plants over Time

Some kinds of plants have been around for a long time. Ferns were around when dinosaurs were alive. Ferns still live all over the Earth, growing and germinating new ferns. Some kinds of plants no longer exist and will never live on Earth again. Those plants are now **extinct.** A type of living thing that once lived on Earth but never will again is extinct.

We can learn about extinct plants by studying their **fossils.**
A fossil is the remains or traces of an animal or plant from a long time ago. Fossils get left behind in rock.

Fern fossil

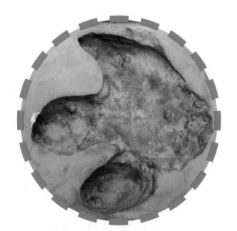

Dinosaur footprint

A fossil can be a footprint a dinosaur made in mud that over time hardened into rock.

Or it can be a plant leaf that has been pressed into layers of mud. After millions of years, the mud hardens into rock, which contains a print of the plant leaf.

Leaf fossil

Plants have changed over time. The earliest plants had spores instead of seeds. Spores are tiny, round, and much smaller than seeds.

Plants have changed as the Earth has changed. Coniferous trees now grow in many places. Flowering plants have been on Earth for a much shorter time than plants with spores. But they can now be found almost anywhere.

Today there are many different types of plants. Without plants, no other living things would be able to exist on Earth. Plants make the sugars that animals use as food to eat and grow.

Plants turn carbon dioxide into the oxygen that we breathe. They make seeds for new plants with cones or flowers, and often use animals, wind, and water to help them reproduce.

Now, after reading this book, you know the facts. Plants are amazing!

Glossary

coniferous   a plant that makes seeds in a cone

deciduous   a plant that loses its leaves in the fall and grows new ones in the spring

extinct   no longer lives on Earth

fossil   the hardened remains or traces of plants or animals

germinate   when a plant starts to grow

pollinate   when pollen is moved to the part of the flower that grows seeds

seed leaf   part of a seed that has stored food for a young plant

seedling   a plant that has just started to grow roots and a stem

system   a group of parts that work together